Study Advice

Improving the Process of Gaining Knowledge

Robert Davis

CS

Claystone Studies

Publication Date: February 2025

ISBN: 978-1-966718-00-0 (Paperback)
ISBN: 978-1-966718-01-7 (Hardback)
ISBN: 978-1-966718-02-4 (eBook)
ISBN: 978-1-966718-03-1 (Audiobook)

Library of Congress Control Number: 2025931946

Published by Claystone Studies.

For more information, visit: claystonestudies.com.

Note: Readers are responsible for any actions they take based on the information or advice in this book. Like every individual, the author has both knowledge and ignorance and makes mistakes and errors from time to time.

Table of Contents

Preface

This book is offered to all learners and students for the purpose of helping them improve their studying process and thus attain greater success in their studies and lives. The book is relevant for learners of a wide range of ages and states of life.

The act of studying occurs whenever we genuinely intend to learn something. Therefore, the study advice in this book is for all those who seek to improve their process of gaining knowledge.

The advice offered is clear and direct. It is also realistic, substantive, and effective. This study advice can bear good results, I believe, when put into practice.

As always, it is important for individuals to exercise their independent judgement and scrutiny when encountering material offered by others. Readers should take responsibility for any actions they take based on the information or advice in this book. Like every individual, I have both knowledge and ignorance and make mistakes and errors from time to time. At the same time, my intention is to communicate truth and promote the genuine good and success of all readers.

I offer my best wishes for all those who seek to practice and actualize the guidance and information in this book.

1. Understand what the purpose is

First, you must understand what the purpose of your studying is. "Why am I doing this?" You need to get clear on this in order to properly integrate your studies into your life as a whole. Otherwise, your studies may feel like a disconnected element in your life, a group of obligations that you despise.

In general, it is not good to do something without knowing why you are doing it. "What is the end goal of this activity?"

In order for this to work, it will be important to become aware of your own goals and purposes that you have in your own life. Then, you will be able to tie your studies into the overarching goals of your life. But if you do not have an idea of what you are aiming for in life, it will not be easy to integrate your studies into something that is your own—your life.

Let's work with an example. Michael is interested in becoming a lawyer. He believes in promoting justice, fairness, and order in the world, and judges that a career as a lawyer will be an effective means to do so.

We can break down his goals into three. Goal (1) is the last goal, and goal (3) is the beginning goal.

It is wise to set the final goal as goal number one. Let the final goal always be number one—let this be unchanging in your goal system. The final goal is your unchanging destination, and so, in your goal-setting procedure, let the number assigned to your final goal be unchanging.

This helps to reduce the number of unnecessary steps to the final goal. If you could immediately dwell in the attainment of the final goal, you would do so. It is only due to various suboptimal conditions—imperfections, non-ideal conditions—that you have to work with intermediate goals in the first place. Therefore, let this fact be reflected in your goal-setting procedure.

To the extent possible, participate as much as possible in your final goal, now. Why wait, if it is truly your final goal? Here, you can do a reality check with yourself: "Do I really hold this to be my final goal? If so, I will be eager, in this moment, to participate in it as much as possible." If you find that your activity does not actually correspond to your understanding about your goals, then either correct yourself and make yourself more authentic, or perhaps go back to the drawing board and identify what your goals actually are. Or, perhaps you *are*, in fact, moving toward your final goal, but in a way that does not correspond to your usual conceptual framework. Judgement and discernment are required.

Now, back to the example with Michael. His end goal, step (1), is promoting the vitality and welfare of his country and the world, and this includes the vitality and welfare of himself, as well. His intermediate goal, step (2), is to promote justice, fairness, and harmony in his community. His immediate goal, step (3), is to become a lawyer for this purpose. To summarize, Michael intends to (3) become a lawyer (2) to support justice in his community, for the ultimate purpose of (1) promoting the happiness and common good of the world.

Now, in order to become a lawyer, he must first attend law school and pass the proper legal examinations. And for this, he must successfully graduate college. So, these are two additional goals: graduating college and graduating law school. We can notate these goals and integrate them as follows: Michael must (5) graduate college, (4) graduate law school, and then (3) become a lawyer.

So, when Michael encounters his studies in high school after having thought about these things, he is now in a position to integrate his studies and make them his own. He will not fall into the trap of thinking that he is doing his studies out of mere obedience to others, like a blind servant. Instead, he will understand that these studies—in English class, biology, history, math, and so forth—are empowering him to attain his highest human potential, which means, his highest happiness. He understands that his happiness consists in offering genuine service to the world and attaining his own highest potential, and that his studies—the knowledge he is gaining—is directly equipping him to do this.

It is difficult to see, sometimes, that your studies are giving you *independence*, since we may do our studies in circumstances where we are dependent on others in certain ways. But in fact, your mind is who you are, and your mind is the perpetual seat of your independence. So, Michael proceeds with his studies, having this knowledge, and is able to weather the storms that come his way, since he understands that gaining knowledge through his studies is directly linked with attaining his potential as a human being. And that is non-negotiable—you demand to attain your human potential, just as you insist on seeking what is good for yourself, because there is no difference between the two.

2. Looking more deeply into purpose

The previous chapter looked at purpose with an example featuring Michael. This chapter will examine the deeper nature of purpose in human life. This chapter will have a three-part framework: the final goal, interests, and money.

(1) Final goal. All living beings move toward life. They seek life. This is the nature of things. Life can mean the state of being alive, and it can also mean vitality. The second sense—vitality—is what we mean when we say that some person we know is "full of life." Vitality means well-being. Vitality is genuine value and utility. For example, products in the economic marketplace do well if they genuinely contribute to vitality and well-being in a person's life.

There is an unchanging goal for all humans. This simply *is* the goal for all humans; humans do not create this goal, but identify it. The goal is this: *life,* or equivalently, *vitality*, for the community and the individual, but primarily, for the community. Life for the community includes life for the individual.

How can it be demonstrated that life for the community is primary, and life for the individual is secondary in importance? Through a common-sense thought test. If we said, "There is complete life and vitality in this community," this would be a sufficient accomplishment. For, all of the individuals are included in the concept of community. But if we said, "There is complete life and vitality for this individual," we would still wonder about the state of the community. This is the *logical* order of importance, in the objective order of things—first community, and second, any particular individual. But for the individual—in the perspective of the individual—the *temporal* order of importance is to generally secure its own vitality and welfare first, just as one must first obtain a sufficient education or knowledge base, through some means, before one can serve the society in the most effective manner. Yet each reasonable individual will acknowledge that, objectively speaking, the success and welfare of the community has more weight than the success and welfare of itself. This is the logic underlying the act of offering oneself to the society and its common good, as does, for example, a firefighter, a parent, a nurse, a teacher, a soldier, and so forth.

Knowing this, you can consciously participate, partially, in this final goal at any time, even now. The point of the path, or journey, is that you increase your partial participation in the goal over time. The goal represents the ideal state, to be approached more and more over time, where you *fully* participate in the goal.

Okay, we have discussed the common, final goal for all humans —vitality. (Final goal, here, means primary, fundamental, and core goal.) This signifies health, flourishing, and happiness in the body, mind, and being of each individual, and the same for the community as a whole—health, flourishing, and happiness. Most everyone will ultimately agree that they seek these things; that the final goal for all humans *is* vitality is, therefore, an uncontroversial claim. Controversy and disagreement arise about *how* vitality for humans is to come to be; but *that* vitality and flourishing, in all relevant respects, *is* the common goal for all humans is difficult to dispute. (Why is life—human life—called life? As in, when we say, "Life is good," or, "What should we do in life?" In my view, life is called life because life is for the sake of life.)

(2) Interests. Now, let us discuss the second topic: interests. There are an infinite number of human interests. (Within the category of interests, in this framework, are all of the intermediate goals humans may have that ultimately lead to the final goal of vitality discussed above.) What is an interest? The word 'interest' traces to the Latin words 'inter' (between) and 'esse' (to be, to exist). So, an interest means that an individual combines its being with something. You shape your being toward an activity. The activity draws your being into *it*. You enter into an activity space. You let your mind take on the shape of the activity.

Let us take a moment to regroup our thought: human life is about moving toward the final goal of vitality, for the individual and community, generally through our interests. There is one final goal, or purpose: vitality. And there are an infinite number of possible interests, the ways we may genuinely actualize our being in space and time.

What determines what interests you have? Things like your experience, your attributes, and your understanding. But it is primarily your understanding that determines what interests you have. (This shows the importance of study.) Why is this? Why is it that your understanding determines what interests you have?

You first have to know that something *is* good before you pursue it *as* good. For example, you must know that spinach *is* good for digestive health before you pursue spinach *as* good, buying it at the grocery market. Any interest you might have around spinach, like cooking it in various ways, discussing it with friends, or doing more research into it, first depends on your understanding that spinach *is* good. The understanding determines the interest.

This point is missed by many people—that your understanding determines what interests you will have. This is a crucial point that should be understood to live the best life possible. One should take the time to study the nature of life and the world. "What *are* the good things in life?" One should take this question seriously and spend time on it, since whatever your understanding is about the answer to that question, will determine what you do for the rest of your life. Whatever understanding you have about the answer to that question, indeed, will determine—consciously or subconsciously, yet inevitably—what you do for the rest of your life.

Many people enter into interests that are in their environment and experience. Unfortunately, they do not work deeply and independently with the question, "What *are* the good things in life?" If they did, they would be able to expand their possibilities— approaching the limit of possibility—and go beyond the boundaries of their local environments. With this question, you are able to approach the limit of possibility, because the intelligence is engaging with a universal question that applies to all of human life.

Here are some examples of interests. Perhaps spend three seconds with each example, getting a solid conception of it before moving to the next one, so that going through the examples becomes a contemplation of the potential range of human activity. Building, singing, trading, advising, doing music, reading, observing, cleaning, organizing, greeting, conversing, observing the art of medicine, guarding, protecting, interacting, speaking, discerning, observing and practicing the law, creating, making, caring for, drawing, enjoying, driving, flying, digging, administering, showing, dancing, exercising, thinking, imagining, reflecting, sitting, meditating, contemplating, nourishing, coding, and researching.

The way the term is being used in this chapter, an interest signifies a deep activation of your being toward an activity; your entire self is combined with an activity. An interest, understood here, is not just a light engagement with something. In addition, in certain circumstances it may not be possible to activate one's interests, after a period of independent judgement and contemplation, in a way that would be ordinarily done during times of peace and stability; this may be the case during times of social turmoil, national emergency, or war.

(3) Money. So, we have discussed the final goal and interests. Finally, money is the third topic in the framework of this chapter, which is examining purpose in a deeper manner.

Let us recall the framework. There is the **end goal** and **interests**. The end goal is vitality for the community and for oneself. (The genuine vitality of the individual benefits the community, and the genuine vitality of the community benefits the individual.) Since the individual is included within the whole community as a part, it is possible to simplify and say that the end goal is vitality for the community, the whole. Vitality is happiness. The interests are the many different kinds of possible human activity.

The human being does an interest, where the end goal of all possible interests is to promote the vitality—the life and happiness —of the community and oneself. The interests may be any possible human activity, as long as it is consistent with promoting that end goal. Remember that the end goal—vitality—is not something we create. Rather, this goal, or endpoint of activity, is something that already exists, based on the nature of reality. (All living beings naturally seek vitality, life, and well-being. Happiness is a loose term for this. No living being wills its own non-existence for its own sake.)

So, you have the final goal, and you have your interests. For the sake of simplicity, let us suppose that you are working with one main interest. Now, you have the option of pursuing this interest (a) in combination with the activity of making money or (b) separate from the activity of making money. Either path may be appropriate and fitting in different situations. Good judgement is needed. However, since the necessity to make money is difficult or impossible to avoid, you will have to make money if you wish to be financially independent. And clearly, it is better to make money through an interest, rather than in a way that does not harmonize with your nature.

Now, what is money? Money is the stuff that you pay for things with. If person A sells four mangos to person B, then person B pays eight dollars to person A, in this example. Both feel satisfied. But person A gave away four mangos—person A feels satisfied because money truly represents value, due to an agreement made among people in the society. It was agreed upon: "These paper bills shall represent value; they may be traded as a medium of exchange." Money is a medium of exchange. Value is not powerful because of money; money is powerful because of value. Value is powerful because of itself.

So, money represents value. One may wish to dismiss the value of money completely. However, in this world, the bodily elements of food and shelter may be obtained using money. It may be possible to do without formal shelter, but for human beings with physical, human bodies, it is not possible to do away with food. Therefore, even if one has adopted a mental and values-based approach to reduce the value of money in one's perspective, it will generally not be possible to eliminate the value of money completely in one's perspective and belief system. Generally, money will always register with some degree of physiological force in your consciousness, since money is connected with the physiological requirement of acquiring food to merely survive. In other words, if you have money, you will be able to purchase food. And you cannot get over this need to eat food. So, you will always affirm the proposition, "Money signifies value," either consciously or subconsciously.

In my understanding, the only scenario where money could register as having *no* value to someone would be the hypothetical scenario where the individual hypothetically existed as a spirit without a material body, and so, where the physical items of food and housing would be unnecessary for the continued existence of the individual. Otherwise, it seems to me, money will inevitably register as having value to every human intelligence, in proportion, for example, to the hunger that arises when one has not eaten in the day up to 3 pm, or in proportion to the aversion one has to sleeping at night without sufficient protection from the cold and rain. This point is important to understand. This is not a pessimistic conclusion. It simply indicates that for every human being, the factor of money should be intentionally addressed and integrated, with intelligence and harmony.

Therefore, it is wise to address this factor of money, instead of pushing it aside on the premise that it has no value whatsoever. Even if you tell yourself that money has no value, you will believe, consciously or subconsciously, that money has value, since it can at least be used to acquire food, and every human being needs food. This also applies to shelter or housing, but I am focussing on the example of food to clarify the point.

This is the reason why great stress and anxiety may arise in one's mind, body, and being around the factor of money. The factor of money is connected to the bodily sense of survival. The value of money is at least admitted or affirmed subconsciously, and this subconscious affirmation of the value of money may produce stress and a festering in one's consciousness, particularly, for example, when the conscious layer of one's mind is not facing the problem of money head on—the problem which the subconscious layer of the mind knows about. This dissonance produces stress and anxiety. The dissonance occurs when your subconsciousness knows there is some problem about money in your life, but your surface consciousness is not properly addressing and resolving the issue.

Ultimately, the subconscious anxiety about money will persist in some degree, great or small, as long as an individual is living on this earth, for there is always some uncertainty about whether human collective cooperation will continue or dissolve, and human collective cooperation is a condition for the continued value of money, and even for the assurance that one's material resources will remain properly protected and secure. The main solution, in my understanding, to reduce this underlying fear and stress, is to genuinely and consistently contribute to the collective human flourishing, so as to always promote the conditions of harmony, stability, and happiness among humanity.

There is an opposing view, which says that for acquiring the bodily necessities of life, personally acquiring money does not have to be necessary, due to the reality of mutual human support. Humans support one another. One can receive the required material elements, such as food and shelter, through the compassionate support of others, in one form or another.

To a degree, this is true and valid. However, the factor of money is not eliminated; it is just pushed back one level. One becomes dependent on others, who themselves earn and receive money in order to support the first person. This does not seem to be the ideal, to the extent that being independent, autonomous, and free are ideals in human life. Generally, if we do not ourselves earn money, then we will become dependent on others who *do* earn money. Then, we will be dependent on those others, and they will have some degree of control over us, and we will be subject to their values, which may change or even degrade over time. This does not seem to be the ideal way to live as a human being in this world. Attaining maximum independence—where one attains the strongest foundation upon which to live joyfully, serve others, and contribute to a flourishing world—seems to be an essential element of an ideal human life.

The conclusion is that money should be consciously and wisely addressed in one's life in order to maximize one's independence and joy in this world, where one has a physical, bodily existence and where there exists a money economy. However, the imperative to make money is not a pessimistic reality. As I will explain below, the imperative to make money is a true occasion to participate in the maximum potential of human existence, just as much as if this world did not have a money economy.

Money signifies value, based on an agreement that the individuals of a society have made with themselves. If you have a stack of three $20 bills on your table, it has been agreed that those $20 bills represent value, such that you can give those bills to the grocery store in exchange for a certain group of food items, which have value—the food offers your body nutrition and permits you to continue living.

The grocery store is receiving money from *you* because the grocery store is giving you value. In this case, the value is food. So, in order for you to earn and receive money from *others*, the way is to give value to others. The way is to give value to society, to serve society, to uplift others, to contribute to the steady improvement of this world. Do you remember that it was mentioned at the beginning of this chapter, that the final goal of human life is vitality, both for the individual and the community? See how the activity of earning and receiving money ("making money"), when done rightly and according to correct principles, is directly a participation in the final goal of human existence—contributing to life and vitality for the whole, in which each individual is included as a part.

Now, there is a potential distinction between objective value (real value) and perceived value. In other words, in a society, it is possible that the value judgements of the people do not correspond to the actual facts about (i) what things are valuable and (ii) to what degree. This mismatch between people's judgements about value, and what is actually the case about value, may be great or small.

In fact, all intelligences are finite and have limits, and so there will always be a separation between objective value and perceived value. For example, if humans only had perfect judgements about value, then no errors or mistakes in action would be made at any time. We can see that this is not the case: human civilization on the earth is partially characterized by disorder and dissonance. We also have a sufficient approximation of the standards of perfection, to correctly make the judgement that our judgements about value often do not correspond to what is objectively the truth about value. In other words, we could not *know* that we weren't getting it right regarding our values if we did not at least have a faint idea of some higher standards of perfection. (Interestingly, this shows the immanent possibility of improvement among ourselves, so long as we have the determination and willpower to do so: we sense and intuit the way.) Thus, it is shown that among hypothetical communities of rational agents, and certainly among humans on this planet, there are various degrees of separation between perceived value and objective value, due to the limitations of finite intelligences operating in time.

Therefore, the principle of making money is that you should offer an objective good to the world and show *that* it is an objective good. (Showing *that* the good is, in fact, a good, is the ideal of marketing, done rightly and ethically. Marketing means, and should be understood to mean, helpfully communicating the truth about something beneficial.) You have to bridge the values. You have observed some particular thing to be good for humanity, but humanity may not adequately perceive the truth that this thing *is* good, objectively speaking. So, you show humanity that it is, in fact, good, correctly bridging the values. Doing this, you earn money, as other individuals offer you value for the value you are offering them.

And it works both ways. It would be incorrect to suppose that you are in a completely superior position, and the rest of the people, the market, are in an inferior position. Remember that every person has interests. In respect to the specific interest that an individual has, that individual will often have a better understanding of its nature and value, due to the time and energy the individual has put into the interest, and the direct experiences gained while doing the interest. So, you will tend to have a superior insight into the value of something associated with your interest, while you will be in an inferior position concerning all of the other interests and goods about which others have gained insights and you have not. In a society, learning and teaching alternate organically: person A learns from person B who functions as a teacher at one time, and then, person B learns from person A who functions as a teacher at another time.

Let us summarize. On this planet, there is a money economy. (The word 'economy' essentially means how people relate to each other. On this earth, money is part of how people relate to and exchange with each other. Possibly, in other hypothetical civilizations in other parts of the universe, physical money is not a part of how the individuals relate to each other.) Money signifies value. In other words, money functions as a symbol of value, or goodness. Indeed, in principle, money functions as a symbol of goodness. (Do not become pessimistic at this point. Remember that there is a distinction between objective value and perceived value. This accounts for how lots of money can become associated with activity that is unwholesome or even malicious—it is due to misunderstandings about value.) Now, in order to obtain things of value, you have to give things of value—giving and receiving, the principle of balance. In a money economy, the thing that you give, in exchange for receiving the value, is money. In this way, money is a medium of exchange. Food and housing are included among the things that are exchanged for money. Thus, it is difficult or even impossible to get out of the necessity to earn money, if one wishes to be fully independent and empowered. And to earn money, the procedure is to provide a good to others and, if appropriate, to show that it is a good, if they do not perceive the goodness of the thing you are providing.

Now, in the process of providing a good to others, it is possible to proceed in two different ways. The second way is better than the first. In the first way, you work with the perceived values among the market as the only realities, even when you have an insight or understanding that the actual, objective value of the things in question is different. This way may involve laziness or cowardice. In the second way, you stay true and authentic to your understanding of reality and seek to offer to the market what, in your understanding, is *actually and objectively* good, not merely what is *perceived* to be good. (People may perceive some things to be good, which actually are not, through unwholesome habit and lack of care in discernment.) This second way involves more energy and courage. Ultimately, the second way grants an individual more money, since money correlates with value—once the people in the market recognize *that* what the individual is offering is something excellent, something better than before, they will offer the appropriate amount of money that corresponds with the increased value of the good.

In other words, objective value is the foundation of perceived value. Perceived value is *not* the foundation of objective value. (If you perceive a stone to be nutritious, it does not become nutritious. If you do not perceive some blueberries to be nutritious, they are still nutritious.) So, if a seller offers something that is objectively better than what has come before, this will eventually be recognized, even if it does not align with the expectations and understandings of the potential buyers in the beginning. Thus, it is shown that seeking to conform to objective value, rather than perceived value, is both wiser and more practical, although it requires more energy and courage.

Working only with perceived value leads to less fulfillment. But acknowledging objective value, and the real possibility of communicating the truth and reality of this objective value, leads to joy and fulfillment in the activity of making money.

Let us do an example. Imagine a time shortly after the printing press was invented in Europe in the 1400s, where books could now be printed in large volume and did not have to be handwritten every time. Imagine that you were involved in the development of the printing press in some meaningful way. Now, you wish to share the benefit of the printing press with other communities, in exchange for receiving money. Seeking to sell the printing press, you travel to a certain kingdom. This kingdom has a large community of scribes who live close to their imperial palace. You seek to sell the printing press to this community of scribes. Initially, they do not see the value in the printing press, and are even averse to it, because the scribes fear that if many people have books, then the writing services of the scribes will no longer be regarded as valuable. This is their perceived value. But you understand, and have the insight, that the objective value of things does not entirely match up with their mistaken perceived values. You understand that if the people directly engage with books, the people's interest in the knowledge of the scribes will increase, leading to a greater demand for their services in other areas, aside from writing. So, you communicate this insight to the scribes, and eventually the scribes come to recognize the truth of your position, and they purchase one of your printing presses. And it came to be that when the printing press was installed there, the scribes were more valued in the kingdom, and were engaged in even more literary activities, due to the literary interest of the people increasing as they directly and personally encountered more books. This concludes the example.

Now, it may be possible to pursue your main life interest separately, at least for a certain time, unconnected to the economy.

Whether you do will depend on your individual circumstances and judgement. But since an economy signifies the relations among people, it will be difficult or impossible to live separately from the economy altogether, at least to the extent that you require food, and the cultivation and production of food involve a collective effort. So, if appropriate in your case, when you are seeking to offer a good associated with your interest to the market, you can seek to make a bridge, through communication, between your recognition of objective value and the perceived values and awareness of the market.

Self-employment is advantageous, because if you are self-employed, you are in a strong position to create that bridge from your unique discovery of value to the current values of society. The internet makes it easier to be self-employed. In other words, if society is not currently paying for the good thing associated with your interest, and you believe that this thing really does have value, an option is to be self-employed, perhaps start a business, and show the people the value in this thing that you have already discovered, for yourself, to be worth your time, energy, and life. Thus, with energy and courage, the activity of making money is a participation in a high purpose of human life—promoting the good of all people. And this itself is roughly the final goal of all activity for any human being—the promotion of, and participation in, life and vitality, for oneself and, more primarily, the whole community of individuals.

In conclusion, this chapter examined purpose more deeply. The framework had three parts: **(1) final goal, (2) interests**, and **(3) money**. The final goal of human life, vitality, is generally to be pursued through your interests. Aside from those cases where, for a variety of possible reasons, you do not need to make money, you intelligently integrate the necessity to make money with your interests, where making money means providing genuine value to society, where society recognizes that what you are providing *is* valuable. Good communication is the means to foster this recognition. Making money—more precisely, receiving money—should be a joyful and meaningful activity, because it is about seeking and encountering objective truth and goodness and sharing that truth and goodness with the whole community. Understanding this framework, you will be able to orient and perform your studies more skillfully, having a better sense of context and direction about the purpose of human life.

3. Knowledge is independent of your circumstances

There is a distinction between (1) the knowledge that you gain and (2) the setting and circumstances in which you gain it.

The knowledge that you gain is universal. You can get such knowledge in any number of places and circumstances. It is only the setting and circumstances that are particular.

It is possible to make the mistake of devaluing the knowledge to be gained simply because you do not like the surrounding circumstances, such as the school environment, the classroom, the teachers, and so forth. However, it is important to understand that the knowledge is independent and universal—the math in math class, the biological information in biology class, the historical information in history class, the logic in critical thinking class, the creative writing principles in English class. The teacher did not invent that knowledge; the teacher related the knowledge as an intermediary.

Therefore, knowing this, have enthusiasm and eagerness to amass such knowledge in your classes and elsewhere. Nobody owns knowledge, and knowledge directly benefits you. Become your own master in your studies, just as you are your own master in the other things you personally do in life.

4. Looking outside the established resources

You may encounter a pre-determined curriculum, with certain resources already decided for you, in your school, professional, or other environments, in a situation where you are supposed to learn about a topic. Before jumping into those resources and fully engaging with them, it will probably benefit you to do some preparatory steps first, outside of the established curriculum resources. This will assist you in taking ownership of the learning process of the topic in question.

First, explore your intuitions. Sit in silence and simply consider the subject matter in an easygoing way. The intention is to let your mind naturally think about the subject matter. Points will be spontaneously organized in your mental space. This is a productive activity, even though it may seem that not much is going on. What is happening is that you are getting mentally settled and organized in the space of the subject matter.

Value your initial understanding of the topic. There may be the tendency the dismiss your initial understanding, since you believe that you know basically nothing about the topic. However, you probably know more about it than you believe you do. Offer deep respect for whatever initial understanding or knowledge you have about the topic, and become aware of it. This will help you; it can only help you, since you are increasing in self-awareness, which is always a good thing. But it is difficult to do. It requires discipline.

Then, before fully engaging with the resources of your curriculum—a school curriculum, a business curriculum, or whatever it is—consider what *you* would do if you wanted to learn about this topic. What would you do if you needed to learn the topic in a few days and a lot of pressure was on the line? You might call this your *go-to way.*

For example, if you are learning physics, your go-to way might be to watch four videos on the topic and then read the introductions of two online encyclopedia articles. After having done this, you would have a solid grasp of the basic framework of the topic. If you had to learn about the topic in two days, this might be your natural approach. Therefore, in your academic or professional setting, using this approach before you engage with the assigned curriculum would be helpful. It would be enlightening and empowering.

If you are taking classes, you will likely be assigned certain textbooks to read. So, in addition to these, it is useful to read other resources, as well. For example, you might find that your textbook is written by just one author, who unfortunately, has chosen to include shallow humor or frivolous anecdotes in the chapter introductions, for example, trying to distinguish themselves as an author. When visiting the Wikipedia page for the same topic, however, you find that you encounter an excellent overview of the essence of the subject in just the article's introduction, something you have been subtly craving all along, as you suddenly understand the basic framework of the subject.

Using just your assigned textbook can lead you into the feeling, the attitude, that you are just obeying the rules in your studies—that you are just following the program established by others. It is not an example of taking your learning into your own hands; of taking ownership of your learning. When you take full responsibility for your learning, new energy opens up in your studies, and your study and learning feel more vital to your life.

Therefore, in addition to properly understanding your assigned textbook, it is good to use your intuition and discover what other resources will give you better vantage points in the subject. Some examples of using other resources include: reading some Wikipedia articles, listening to a podcast, watching some relevant videos, or reading a different book on the topic that interests you.

In addition, doing this will give you confidence in your classes, as you will step into the classroom with a deeper understanding of the material than your peers. You will have more vantage points, more perspectives, and a better understanding of the framework of the subject, not just as elaborated by your textbook author, but as understood by the common expert consensus of humanity, which is a more important standard.

Whatever learning environment you are in, consult your independent judgement to scan the opportunities and resources outside of the established curriculum, in order to maximize the chances of forging connections between your unique nature and the resources available in the global sphere.

5. Breaking things down

If you encounter something complex or difficult to understand, you may break it down. Everything can be broken down into its simple parts.

You may be averse to this method because it requires a lot of diligence, care, and patience. However, it is worth doing. You will likely find the solution to the problem faster than if you avoided this method for the reason that it was too hard.

This method is like being asked to pick up a lady bug from a leaf when you are running quickly on a track. The plant is next to the track and you are nearly out of breath running. Before you can deftly and appropriately deal with the plant, you have to stop, take some breaths, and recollect yourself into a state of poise and balance. Then, you can skillfully take the ladybug off the leaf.

It is the same with doing the method of breaking down a difficult problem or concept into its simpler parts. You must pause, perhaps take some deep breaths, recollect yourself, and then direct your intelligence to breaking down the complex thing into its simple parts.

One mistake that is possible to make here is to falsely judge: "This is very hard, whereas it should be easy. I'm not going to do it, since this is embarrassing." It is true that it is very hard, but it is *not* true that it should be easy. Breaking things down is one of the most difficult things in the world. You have to know *what* the simple parts are. This is the basic method and project in all the sciences, for example—breaking down the complex world into its simpler parts, ultimately understanding the laws and principles at the foundation of the subject matter. Obviously, this is *still* a work in progress in many areas of human knowledge, like physics. So, breaking complex things down into their simpler parts is a simple process, but it is difficult to do. But even a little progress in this direction goes a long way toward producing real wisdom and knowledge in the subject matter.

6. Going slowly

There is an old saying: "Slow is smooth, and smooth is fast." Beware of the general tendency to try to go quickly through your studies when you have a lot on your plate. Often, what you need the most is to slow down, taking everything slowly. Going slowly allows your subconscious mind to orient and ground itself without being bombarded by the anxiety of having to do an unrealistic number of tasks in an unrealistic amount of time. If you give room to this type of anxiety, then your mind cannot accurately define the problems that need to be solved. And yet, accurately defining problems is precisely the path to solving them.

Therefore, whenever you are facing difficulties in your studies, *going slowly* can serve as a successful path forward. There is another way to think about this. It is not so much about going quickly or slowly. It is about going *at all*. It is about moving forward *at all*. Our studies fail when we stop doing them *at all*, and instead, for example, move to another task in despair, frustration, or abandonment. This sense of despair, frustration, or abandonment can be very subtle and quick in our consciousness. It can occur for a very brief moment, right before we actually make the decision, consciously or subconsciously, that we are going to stop our studies.

Many times, our concept of what it means to *move forward* in our project or activity involves a disordered expectation—we may think that to move forward means to proceed with great speed and high skill. If we do not reach those bars, then we abandon the idea of moving forward at all. This is a mistake.

All that is needed is to *move forward in any way at all.* Moving forward *slowly* allows us to do this in a way that is realistic and attainable. Ironically, once we start moving forward again in a slow and accessible manner, things settle back into more clarity in our consciousness, and we might even find ourselves going rather quickly through our studies, tasks, and activity. This is because our mind has had the chance of gaining clarity and definition about the situation at hand.

Once you do get into the flow again, you do not always have to go slowly through things. You might find that going quickly through your studies, at certain times, is beneficial and natural. However, when you feel difficulties arising and encounter obstacles moving forward, *going slowly* may be a valuable tool.

7. Doing some breathing before studying

Getting increased oxygen into the body has powerful effects not only for the body, but for the mind and intuition as well. Therefore, doing some conscious breathing exercises before your studies can increase your capacity and potential to go deeper and have more clarity and satisfaction in your studies.

Your breath is related to your mind, and your mind is related to your breath. For example, in a certain situation, the mind believes that there is some kind of danger around, and the breath changes accordingly, becoming shorter and stronger. (Remember that belief is an operation of the mind. In this example, the mind's understanding determined the state and quality of the breath.) Likewise, everyone has experienced that after doing some deep breaths, the mind has more peace and clarity.

The difficulty is to consciously do the deep breathing in the appropriate situations, making the decision to do so. There is the general tendency to skip this step and just dive into the study activity—or problem, more generally—without allowing ourselves to receive the benefits of the disciplined procedure of conscious breathing exercise. The discipline is a key, here—one must have great discipline in order to pause, do some conscious, deep breathing, and *only then* begin one's studies.

If you can practice and achieve the discipline required to do this, this discipline will naturally benefit other areas of your life, as well.

Doing conscious, deep breathing is about *trusting the process*. You are simply engaging in a process that you have control over, without having any disordered expectations about results. You are still aiming for a particular result. I will not say that you have *no expectation*, because that is unrealistic—you have the expectation that you will complete the breathing process, for example, and that doing so will produce an improved quality of being and activity for you. But, your expectations are *more harmonious*, because they are clearer and more defined in your consciousness. Abandoning expectation is not the way, because that means abandoning your individual authority and executive control over your life and activities. Instead, your expectations should be clear, and they should facilitate your success.

8. Discovering an important truth about language

Many problems in your studies may trace to the constructed nature of human language. In other words, many problems in your studies may be due to a problem about communication—a simple difficulty in communicating a concept, where the original intention of the teacher or author was obscured by some arbitrary features of human language.

Here is an example. Suppose you are reading a book in your English class. The author has a particular intuition and imagination about a certain character, but unfortunately, the author uses disorganized and confused language to portray the character. As a result, the original intention for the character is lost in the way that the character has actually come to be described in the book. It is as if the author had a perfectly clear experience of the character in imagination, but was dealing with a certain code—the human language—using which the original clarity of the character became diluted and lost.

The way that humans naturally interact with the world, using the mind and senses, is *unconstructed* and *uncreated*. It is simply a part of nature. All humans, no matter their background or culture, encounter objects in the world with their five senses and process these realities with their minds. However, every human language, such as English, Greek, Chinese, Italian, Spanish, and so forth, is *constructed* and *created*. It came to be at a certain point in time, and it was created by humans. Any particular language is not an inevitable and natural part of human experience. Particular human languages can either be or not be, without affecting the natural operations of humans with their five senses and minds.

A fundamental point is that *created* human languages trace to the *uncreated* and *unconstructed* nature of human experience. In other words, all constructed human languages, like English, Italian, Spanish, Russian, and so forth, trace to a common communication and experience. This is the natural experience of human consciousness interacting with the world through the five senses and the mind. This natural experience also involves the feelings of the heart, which are universally experienced among humans, such as attraction and aversion, happiness and sadness, harmony and disharmony, and peace and anger.

When we experience something in the world, first there is the immediate intuition in our consciousness, which is prior to any human language. Our senses receive the data from the world, and the data from the senses is assembled as a smooth, coherent experience in our mind. This experience is an intuition. The reality of this experience, this intuition, does not require any human language in order to exist. It is an original, intuitive experience. This intuition contains a lot of data and information. It is only after the experience of this intuition that we use the elements of a constructed, human language, like English or Chinese, in either (1) our own thinking in our own minds or (2) in our communications with others.

This is an important key in your studies. Whatever author you are reading, or whatever subject you are studying, will be expressed in a particular human language. But all human languages trace to the same source—nature. The immediate reality of the world is received by the five senses and the mind. Unlike human languages, the five senses and the mind are products of nature. No human created the five senses and the mind.

The instances of original, natural intuition in the mind, which contain lots of information, may then become expressed—well or poorly—through the structures of a constructed, human language, like English, Japanese, or Russian.

So, the forms and expressions that you find in a human language, like English, are not infallible. They are not the end all, be all. They are not the golden standard of knowledge, *even if* they are contained in excellent textbooks. These forms and expressions are secondary. The *primary* elements of knowledge are the intuitions of the mind when it encounters the world through reason and the senses.

Knowing this, if you encounter difficulties in interpreting something in your studies, you may take the independent route of asking, querying, inferring, and investigating, "Where is the author coming from? What essential truth, experienced in natural intuition, is the author attempting to express in this constructed language?"

You may even attempt to recreate for yourself the encounter the author had with the world, think about those truths, and then put the information into words and sentences in a way that is suitable for you. Perhaps your formulation of the information will be inferior, equal, or superior to the author's formulation. But in either of the three cases, your understanding of the material will be better for having done this process. You will have engaged in a process of deeper learning. You are not inventing truth or rejecting objective truth. Rather, you are (1) going some layers deeper than the information expressed in human, constructed language; (2) approaching and examining the same intuitive truth that the author is referring to, and then (3) expressing that same, intuitive truth in words and sentences in the human, constructed language you are working with (English, Spanish, and so forth) in a form that is clearer for you.

8. Discovering an important truth about language

This method promotes a more direct understanding of the material.

9. The obstacle of mental disunity

In your studies, unity is your friend, and disunity is your enemy. I am mainly talking about unity in your mind, but this applies to the unity and harmony of your physical space, too. Unity, in this context, means organization, harmony, and clarity. Disunity means a lack of organization, not knowing what you are doing next, not having a clear list of what needs to be done, and being scattered in general. Indeed, although mental unity is most important, it is also important to have unity and organization in the physical surroundings that you oversee and create. Mental unity and physical unity complement and reinforce each other.

Used poorly, technology can multiply your mental fragmentation. It is important to use technology to your advantage. It is possible to use technology in a way where it actually reduces your power to get things done, skillfully complete tasks, and work effectively. A main way that technology ends up harming you—and the responsibility is yours, since you have control over it—is when you permit yourself to become mentally scattered while using it. Often, this happens when you forget the purpose of why you are doing something, and just get lost in using the technology, acting without purpose, perhaps letting temporary, unplanned interests become your master and guide for your time using the devices.

Temporary, unplanned interests should not be your guide when using technology. An example of a temporary, unplanned interest is this: seeing a random, but captivating, video thumbnail and then getting lost in that rabbit hole, abandoning any original purpose you might have had. If you would like to browse and explore videos, then do so with intention and control. For example: "I will explore videos on this particular topic for 40 minutes." Then, the process of watching videos will have the qualities of clarity, stability, and control. You will maximize the fruitfulness of the activity, instead of proceeding reactively and forfeiting personal autonomy.

What *should* be your guide are conscious intentions and plans that align with your own goals—both your short-term and long-term goals. Then, technology will function as an excellent aid for your highest development. It will serve your advantage, not your disadvantage.

In addition to the way you work with technology, it is important to maximize unity and harmony in as many areas of your life as possible in order to have the most success in your studies. When you sit down to begin your studies, take some time to get clear and settled.

To study well is to engage the whole mind. Lurking problems in your life, even in unrelated areas, register in your mind, and thus will indirectly weigh upon the freedom and dexterity with which you perform your studies. Optimally, therefore, you will attain as much resolution and harmony in your whole life in order to maximize the power of your mind when you engage in the pursuit of knowledge and truth in your studies.

There is a distinction between unity and simplicity. You can still have unity and do many things at once. You can have many things going on at one time in a complex way. But the complex activities should be occurring within a larger harmony, where you have clarity and understanding. In other words, you should never be mentally disunified while engaging in multiple things. Instead, you should always have mental unity, whether you are doing one thing or many things.

9. The obstacle of mental disunity

The path to unity and organization may be different for different people. It is powerful to simply identify the goal of having unity in your life and studies, and then to independently determine the appropriate means to get there—the path that is suitable for you.

10. Lack of focus and restlessness are ordinary qualities

Lack of focus and restlessness are normal, usual, and ordinary qualities in anyone who is attempting to study well.

You may recall the last chapter, which said that mental disunity, metal fragmentation, and mental scatteredness are obstacles to success in studying. So, you might think that this chapter contradicts the previous chapter, since this chapter affirms that these qualities are normal qualities.

However, there is no contradiction. Something can be an obstacle, and yet it can be normal and ordinary at the same time. For example, someone training for a marathon may find that they are getting out of breath too quickly to keep up a good pace to finish the race. Getting out of breath is an obstacle, yes. But getting out of breath is normal and ordinary. There is a normal and ordinary process of improvement.

What is studying? Studying consists in directing our energies to the use of one of the highest faculties we have, our intelligence. This is difficult work. A terrible error to make is to construct an expectation that attaining knowledge in our studies should be smooth and easy. When we do not meet that expectation, we feel despair—even if we do not realize we *are* feeling despair. This despair can occur subtly in our subconsciousness, since we have that expectation that studying should be smooth and easy. Then, we might act from that despair, abandoning our study for some other activity that appears easier to us. (In fact, objectively speaking, our studies might be easier for us than that other activity. It is simply because we don't have any expectation about results with the other activity, that it appears more attractive to us.)

A solution is to make our expectations more accurate. (It is not to eliminate expectation altogether, which is likely impossible to do. Part of being an intelligent being is having some reasonable sense of the future at all times.)

So, we should correctly understand that studying is one of the most difficult activities for any human being. Activating our intellect to cognize objects of pure thought is to approach the border between mind and matter. It is hard work. Mathematics is a prime example of this intellectual work. Numbers are not dependent on physical matter. All studying is some kind of participation in the archetype of mathematical study, since the truths that the intellect apprehends are always abstractions from individual matter to some degree. For example, in biology, when we study the general nature of the cell, we are studying the nature of any possible cell—an abstraction—and not just a particular plant cell in this maple tree over here.

So, we should make our expectations more accurate about the difficulty of studying and the results that are reasonable to expect from our efforts. Doing so is not to condemn ourselves to any particular results in our studying. Moment by moment, we will seek to do the best we can. But this will free us from being hobbled by expectations that are unreasonable.

Here is an example. Mark is preparing to read the last chapter of his assigned book and then write an evaluation essay about the book. Instead of setting the expectation that he will understand all aspects of the last chapter and write an evaluative essay bringing out every essence of the book, he holds a more accurate expectation that in this study session, he will go through the last chapter, probably understand about 80% of the content, and then write a rough draft of the essay, which will cover only certain aspects of the book with a moderate degree of depth.

When Mark begins his studying with this expectation, at the moments when he realizes that he is missing some points in his reading and does not quite understand some details, he does not despair or stop the process, but simply continues reading until the end, since his performance did not contradict any unreasonable standard he set beforehand. Rather, his expectation was *80% understanding*, and missing a few details here and there stands in harmony with that expectation.

In the same way, when Mark begins his essay, he realizes that his essay is a little scattered and that he is having some trouble connecting his thoughts together. If he had too high of an expectation, he might despair and give up at this point, switching to watch some videos on the internet to get some psychological relief. But in fact, his expectation was to cover just *certain* aspects of the book with a *moderate* degree of depth. Overall, his essay is coming along alright, even with the obvious weaknesses that he is noticing in it. But he does not worry about it. He feels calm and content, since he is easily meeting the reasonable expectation he set before.

In the present era, there is a lot of misunderstanding, I believe, about having difficulty focusing and being restless in our studies and academic environments. There are many different ways to learn things. What *is it* that learns? It is the mind. The mind learns. And, the mind is always with us. We *are* our minds. So, we can learn while running, walking, being outdoors, listening to music, doing exercise, lying down, discussing with friends, and in many other ways. Every moment of conscious existence is a potential moment of learning, since we *are* our minds. Even our dreams are potential moments of learning and growth.

Yet, it is a clear truth that our academic environments, in school and college settings, are mostly structured according to a set and concrete way. There is a curriculum, there are desks and chairs, and there are particular methods of teaching and learning that are established within the curriculum. It is not easy to change those structures. So, if an individual learner demonstrates difficulty in focussing, remaining still, or giving attention to the material, there is the tendency to affirm that the thing to be changed is the learner, instead of the learning structures and the environment. Perhaps the school or institution lacks the resources to change the learning structures or implement more programs to connect with different learning styles, and so there is the subconscious motivation to interpret such attention difficulties as a deficiency in the student, instead of as a deficiency in the learning approach, environment, and institutional method. Or perhaps it is embarrassing, painful, and unstrategic—in a business and logistical sense—for the institution to admit that various educational structures, currently in use by convention, require some modification and more flexibility.

It is important to be aware that in situations where the study system and method is concretely fixed for all students, the blame for student difficulties may be shifted onto the students too much. Indeed, we can gain knowledge in outdoor activity, running, looking at things, playing, sitting, reading, and in many other kinds of activities. In every kind of situation while awake, we can gain knowledge, since knowledge is gotten by the mind. (This shows why having good and sufficient sleep is critical for learning and successful studies, since one of the fundamental conditions of learning is having a wakeful and vibrant waking consciousness. As long as you are awake and sharp, the learning process generally happens spontaneously in the mind.)

The mind can do things beyond our expectation. It can handle lots of data being thrown at it in very dynamic environments. Learning does not just have to be sitting down and engaging in steady concentration. The mind is powerful, more powerful than we think. An individual may be playing soccer and yet listen off-and-on, playfully, to a conversation between his teammates about biology class. The next day, the student finds that he deeply retained the information about the biology material. He wasn't even trying. It was just playful, spontaneous activity, entirely natural.

Moreover, our mind operates in cycles. Periods of concentration alternate with periods of expansion and diversification. The learning approach should be able to adapt to these cycles. To regard the individual as having some fault or deficiency during one of the *expansion and diversification* points of the cycle, is simply a misunderstanding. Sometimes concentration comes easy, and sometimes it comes with difficulty or to a minimal degree. This is a natural cycle.

In addition, these cycles may span over different time periods, some short and some long. It is part of our common experience to notice how some individuals were a certain way at one age period, shifted to a different style and disposition some years later, and then again, shifted to a third style some years after that, which yet incorporated some interesting aspects from two periods before. The growth and evolution of a person is cyclical and dynamic; the process will often transcend our comprehension.

Finally, lack of focus and restlessness *will* be present to *some* degree in any human being. The degree will be small or large. These are ordinary qualities. The fact that human beings require sleep demonstrates that our biological capacities are dynamic and require replenishment. We should pursue that style and method of studying that harmonizes with our individual natures, so that the process of studying and learning is as interesting as possible.

11. Long-term life plans benefit your studies

This chapter complements the discussion of purpose in Chapters 1 and 2. Now, it is helpful to make a sketch—at least a tentative sketch—of some long-term life planning before you begin your studies. You may set some short-term and long-term goals through the process of deeply considering your life and identifying goals to aim for. Then, you may configure and orient your studies *within* that larger framework.

One reason this is important is because the activity of gaining knowledge through your studies inherently offers you long-term benefits. Knowledge about different subjects—knowledge of reality in general—does not fade after a few days. If you genuinely learn something, that information contributes to the configuration of your mind, personality, and being for the rest of your life.

Studying, it should be clear, is not just for immediate success in your school environment, general academic environment, work environment, or hobbies, but equips you with power for your entire lifespan. If you do not have a general awareness of your goals in life and what you are aiming for, it will be difficult to engage with your studies in a way that maximally integrates them into *your own* projects and trajectory.

Remember that the knowledge you gain in your studies is independent of its immediate context. You are not studying *for* your teacher, *for* your class, *for* your school, *for* grades, and so forth. (Grades are just indirect metrics for measuring *your own* understanding of the material.) You are ultimately studying for the purpose of gaining knowledge of reality in its various aspects, and the acquisition of such knowledge bestows various benefits in your own life and in the lives of others, such as insights, clarity, organization, innovation, new capacities, and a general expansion of potentiality.

Gaining knowledge of various aspects of reality is to immediately fulfill your own human potential as a rational, intelligent being. There are few activities, other than this, that will make you more independent—intellectually, physically, and logistically. But in order to effectively be aware of these benefits and activate them through the process of study, it will be important to have an awareness of the larger context of your life.

Here is an analogy. You are building a house. Now, in Scenario A, you know exactly what is required for the completion of the house. You know that you require a certain number of kilograms of stone, wood, and cement materials. You know how many construction contractors will be required to complete the job. You know the type of paint that you will use, and the type of plants that will be used for landscaping. Suppose that the house is being built in a town about 30 miles from where you live. Every day, you make the drive to the construction site. Sometimes, as you travel along the road to work, you discover some construction material opportunities along the way. One wholesaler is offering a good deal on cement, and another landscaping company is offering a reasonable price on young trees. *Since you already know exactly what you need and what you are aiming for in terms of the house, you can recognize the opportunities along the road and rightly use them to your advantage.*

Now, imagine Scenario B. You are building the same house, yes, but you have not given any deep thought to its blueprint or to the materials required for the construction project. You daily drive to the construction site out of compulsion, habit, and even slightly from fear about losing the job opportunity, and you follow the general flow of the construction process, adhering to convention without giving it much independent thought. But as you daily drive along the road to the construction site, you miss all of the opportunities presented to you in terms of construction material opportunities. *You recognize none of them, and you utilize none of them, since you have no clear conception of your goal.*

In the same way, if you have clarity about your life plan, direction, and goals, you can successfully integrate your studies into your life to a high degree. If you lack this clarity and vision, the risk is that your study time will be spent inefficiently.

In a similar approach, you may ask yourself, "Have I identified a purpose for my existence?" If you have not identified a purpose through your study of life and nature, then do so—it should be a wholesome purpose that promotes harmony and flourishing for yourself and the greater community.

Then, once you are working with such a purpose, orient your studies according to that purpose. Understand the way in which your studies fit into the larger project and trajectory of your life. Since studying involves learning and knowledge, you will find that studying always traces to the ultimate purpose of your existence.

In other words, studying will always, in one way or another, promote your purpose in life. Why? Studying involves the attainment of knowledge, and most human activities depend on the skillful exercise of intelligence and knowledge.

12. Drafting out your worldview independently

Do you know what your worldview is? Have you established your own, independent views about significant issues concerning human nature, the nature of the world, beneficial ways of living, and human society? Having your own, independent views on these and other subjects, where you arrive at your conclusions through acts of *your own* intelligence, is an essential part of developing your intelligence in the world. It is also an essential part of developing your personality.

Your studying will be enhanced if you come to your studies with some kind of worldview already established—at least in a tentative sense, with working hypotheses. To have a detailed worldview does not have to mean being bigoted, arrogant, or stuck in your ways. That would be having a worldview in a disordered manner. The ordinary and harmonious way of having a worldview is to have particular views and rational accounts for all relevant issues, topics, and fields of knowledge, and at the same time, to understand that there will inevitably be errors in your worldview, due to the limitations of our finite intelligence. You must be vigilant and eager to correct your worldview when better information and rational accounts are encountered, or when false beliefs of yours are noticed that were not noticed before.

Everyone's worldview will contain some degree of flaws and errors, but identifying one's worldview through the hard work of independent investigation, even if it does have errors, is much better than not having this self-awareness and self-understanding at all. Making the initial step of identifying what your understanding is about various aspects of the world is an act that will help you become more established in knowledge.

One may understandingly oppose this recommendation and say, "Why should I make myself to be a carved statue, holding to fixed views? We should be like water—fluid, flexible, ready to adapt, and always sensitive to other perspectives." It is true that all of these are good qualities: being fluid, flexible, ready to adapt, and always sensitive to other perspectives. Here is the key point: identifying your worldview, and drafting it out, is compatible with all of those good qualities. It is a solid exercise to write out on a piece of paper the elements of your worldview. But the words on the paper are secondary. What is primary are the acts of your intelligence as you figure out *what your understandings are* about various things. It is about having an understanding. Your understanding includes the nature of your feelings and intuitions about a certain subject or topic.

It can be tricky, because the idea of "having a view" has two meanings. One meaning is to have an understanding of something; to come to a certain understanding about something. This is the meaning that is meant here, in this chapter—identifying your worldview is about coming to definite understandings about various subjects and topics. These understandings may correspond more or less to the reality of the world. One's understandings are to be improved over time, as one progresses in life. But the initial victory is to determine what one's understandings are. This is an act of self-awareness.

The other meaning of "having a view" is communicating one's understanding in an act of communication with other people. For example, one may state one's view about nutrition to one's friends; one may communicate the view in a print or electronic article. This meaning of "holding a view" is not a necessary or essential part of developing your worldview. Developing your worldview is about identifying and developing your understandings of various topics in life. These understandings will form how you think, speak, and act. Publicly communicating these understandings is not the first instance of power, in this context. The first instance of power is *having* these understandings.

Do you see the benefit and power of developing your worldview? It is about nourishing and activating your mind and your being.

The self-awareness that arises with having a formed worldview enables you to attain more of your potential. One must have some self-awareness in order to work with others with the most skill and capacity as possible. For example, if one is on a dance floor, seeking to dance with others who are also on the dance floor, one must know *where* one is on the dance floor in order to dance skillfully with others. One will be able to receive, flow with, and work with other dancers only if one knows where one is on the dance floor. Similarly, if one has already worked on one's own understanding of a particular topic, one will generally be able to most receptively, welcomingly, and skillfully work with other perspectives on that topic.

One reason for this is that the effort to develop your worldview is the effort to determine *what* is true. It is the effort to determine *whether* something is true or false. It is not really about being happy or upset about things. So, there is no trouble with encountering an infinite number of worldviews. It can all be done in calmness and goodwill. Every human is in the same boat of wanting to know what is true. This is a shared intention. We are all partners in this effort. Even if we have radically contrary views, we still share that intention. (Healing fights and disagreements often involves remembering this truth.)

Negative results can accrue in your studies if you have not done independent work to determine your views—that is, your understandings—about the world beforehand. For example, perhaps you are studying the ancient Roman Empire in your history class. You are reading a perspective about the Roman Empire by a certain author. It is assigned reading for your class. Now, you have not thought about the issue beforehand, and the author offers a persuasive presentation of her view about the reasons why the Roman Empire eventually collapsed in the West. In the course of reading the author's perspective, you simply accept it as your own view, since you had not established a framework for evaluating the issue independently. Whereas, if you had analyzed the issue independently before reading this perspective of the author, you may have ended up arriving at a conclusion distinct from, or opposed to, the author's conclusion. Then, upon reading the author, you would already have had a nurtured foundation from which you could examine and compare the author's data. This would have produced a better understanding of the article; in a certain way, you would have encountered the article with a greater capacity to be receptive, since your understanding would have already been primed. Moreover, you could have integrated any points you judged to be stronger in the author's perspective into your own views, strengthening your understanding.

In an analogy, approaching your studies—or your work in general —without having independently worked on your understanding of the world is like going to the gas station at night. You are on a long road trip, and so the stakes are high. This gas station does not happen to have nighttime lighting. In addition, containers are used; there are no fuel hoses. You put gas into the red gas container. The spout of the red gas container does not automatically fit with the gas tank opening on your car—you have to fit it in with concentration. That night, when you pour the gas, about half of the gas misses the tank and meets the car body, flowing to the ground. In the end, going to the gas station feels inefficient. This is like going to your studies without having previously worked on your independent understanding of the world. Time and energy are spent inefficiently.

To the contrary, approaching your studies with your worldview already identified is like going to same gas station during the day. You funnel the gas from the red container into your vehicle, and all of it enters the tank. You see well because it is daytime. You generally feel satisfied with the experience. You contribute well to the success of your long road trip.

The lesson of the analogy is that if you approach your particular studies after having done the work of identifying and developing your worldview independently, you will most efficiently funnel those studies into your life and existence. You will work with more clarity.

Having an established worldview going into your studies and schoolwork will also help you to see beyond the sting and pressure of grades, and to put them in proper context. Grades are intended to be a measure of your intelligence and understanding of the subjects studied. Your understanding of *those particular* subjects studied, whatever the subjects are, partially contributes to your overall understanding of the world and reality. So, if you all along aim to improve your overall understanding of the world and reality, you will not be tripped up by grades. You are attending to the thing *for whose sake* the grades exist!

There is the legitimate concern that better grades translate into conditions helping you to make money later on. Making money is necessary for your basic survival, and so there is pressure. This is what much of the anxiety and pressure traces to in many school and institutional contexts. (The fight or flight instinct is active.) But who will be examining your grades? High schools, colleges, graduate schools, and perhaps some initial employers, if you decide to get a job after school instead of, for example, starting your own business.

First, if you have been working on establishing your own, independent understanding of reality in an independent way, then when you interview or speak directly to these institutions, your understanding and intelligence will naturally come through, regardless of what your grades happened to be. Second, if your method is to develop your own, independent understanding of reality, then your grades will likely be good, or at least alright, as a natural result of this process.

Your worldview is something that generally persists throughout your whole life—unless, for example, you change it. If you do not consciously develop your understanding of the world, it may be developed passively and by accident. In such a case, you may not like the results, if you were to study what your worldview has become over the course of this passive and accidental process.

The effort to establish your own worldview will enable you to identify areas of life where you have little or no knowledge at all. For example, perhaps you would have never come to understand that you had little knowledge of international relations. But when you asked yourself the question, "What are my views about international relations?" you realized that you knew very little about this subject. To identify things you *don't* know is an excellent accomplishment. Addressing the weakest links in a chain is critical to make the chain stronger.

Finally, if you have done the work of understanding and developing your worldview, you will avoid accepting whatever opinions you happen to encounter in the world, and thus becoming deceived or manipulated. You will be able to test the proposals and propositions that others offer against your tested understandings which have sustained the trial of your inquiry and examination. Having an independent worldview makes you strong and resilient.

13. The benefit of handwriting

Handwriting is an organic process, in a certain way. It is certainly more natural than typing. If you handwrite, you have the opportunity to reflect more deeply on what you are writing. This can be helpful to enter more deeply into your work. Much of the difficulty in writing well is failing to pierce beyond the surface consciousness of the mind. The deeper layers of the mind, and the intuition, contain many insights. Handwriting things offers the occasion to get into these deeper layers.

Handwriting also activates an artistic side of ourselves, particularly if we have the intention to write in an elegant and beautiful way. If we tap into this artistic aspect of ourselves, we can enter an enhanced state of consciousness, from which our thoughts about our writing topic may take on a better form, benefiting from the enhanced awareness necessary to maintain an aesthetic sensibility.

Proceeding in a slow and rhythmical fashion can be an aid for the writing process, in which we aim to offer the best productions of our mind onto the page. Handwriting also allows us to think about what we are writing a second time. First, we have a thought and begin to write it. Second, as we proceed through the motion of writing and complete each word, we have the occasion to think about the meaning again. This natural repetition fosters a deeper contemplation and improves the learning process.

The subconsciousness plays an important role in the writing process. Generally, when working on an electronic platform, the device has the capacity to enable the user to do many different tasks. So, even when writing, opening an internet browser is just a second away, and so is receiving messages in a message application. And the capacity to play sounds, such as music, makes the device able to engage the user with an entirely separate dimension of sensory experience, aside from sight. The subconsciousness, aware of this, always exists in a *potential* state of fragmentation, therefore, when operating such electronic devices for the purpose of writing. The subconscious awareness that one may, at any time, become destabilized from the writing activity may reduce one's performance and depth in writing. It is difficult to enter into the cave of writing when, in the back of your mind, you know that you may be pulled out due to the multiplicity of functions of the computer or electronic device you are using. Handwriting at once removes these possibilities of becoming distracted; handwriting creates a wall of protection around the writing process, which is ultimately an activity of thinking. Since writing is ultimately a thinking process, concentration and distraction are fundamental indications of success and failure.

A large number of the greatest works of literature and philosophy among humanity were handwritten. At a minimum, this shows that handwriting is *consistent* with the production of outstanding masterpieces. Using common sense, we can infer one reason: the activity of handwriting allowed these authors to think deeply without the possibility of becoming distracted in conjunction with a multitasking device.

Compared to typing, handwriting involves more autonomy and activation of intelligence in the following respect, as well. In the activity of typing, each letter is already presented before you on the keyboard. But in handwriting, the letters exist in your mind, and must be distinctly recalled and activated *there* in order for your hand and fingers to write them on the page. This removes a degree of alienation in the writing process and restores your autonomous intellectual activity to a higher position in the writing activity. In addition, the activity of physically writing each letter, as opposed to executing merely the same "button push" motion with your fingers in relation to the corresponding keys, involves more mind and soul; in particular, when writing letters, those regions of your consciousness are activated which are closely related to the identification, discovery, and contemplation of meaning. Thus, handwriting may contribute more to your contemplation of meaning—the substance of your ideas—during the writing process.

14. Opinions and beliefs

Many of your opinions and beliefs are permanent, unless you change them. Thus, it is important to get them right. For, your opinions and beliefs shape your actions and your attitudes. They determine what you do in life and how your life goes. When you look on your life—say, for example, on your deathbed—most of your activities that occurred throughout the decades will have been partial results of your beliefs and opinions.

Your beliefs represent the nature of your understanding of the world. When you attain a deeper knowledge of a certain area in life, you naturally revise your beliefs and opinions accordingly. This revision is like a surge of health in your life, as you think and act according to information that more closely corresponds with the actual nature of the world. It is easy to miss the significance of thus upgrading your beliefs and opinions, but the results are profound.

The activity of studying is an occasion to improve and upgrade your beliefs and opinions about the world. It directly translates into a more empowered, intelligent, and fulfilled existence. Studying brings awareness to your opinions and beliefs, which otherwise may never change throughout your life—or only change a little, slowly, or reactively, as you passively respond to events and the activity of other people. When you study with purpose, you bring the direct force of your intelligence to the storehouse of your beliefs and opinions, and you improve yourself immensely, setting up a better future for yourself and for those whom you impact, in numerous ways, many of which are difficult to comprehend.

When you learn—in cases of true learning—your beliefs often get updated and improved automatically. This is due to the reality of objective truth. Your being contacts the reality of the external world, and you automatically update your beliefs. We should distinguish between cases of true learning and cases of error or false propaganda, where you might quickly change your beliefs without your beliefs corresponding to truth. In the deepest cases of learning, you intuitively feel the truth and substance of the realities in question and your understanding quickly conforms to this new and improved configuration. In this way, skillful studying and learning corresponds with natural and automatic improvements in one's opinions and beliefs.

Your beliefs may be either true or false. One way of framing the quest to reach your highest human potential is this: acquiring true beliefs and removing false beliefs. Why is this twofold activity significant? It is significant because the universe is common and objective, and because objective truth exists. (This is not to say that the objective truth of the universe is easily known. Different people participate differently in knowledge of truth.) Because the objective truth of the universe is something real, whether or not an individual mind corresponds to this objective truth makes a huge difference.

In general, any act of correspondence between one's mind and the objective world is associated with intuition, insight, and success, *to the extent* that such correspondence exists. (One may have a belief structure that partly corresponds to truth and partly does not. This is common and ubiquitous. It is probably the universal fact among humans, as we all have finite intelligences.) Conversely, instances of lack of correspondence between one's mind and the objective world are associated with ignorance, dullness, and failure. Roughly speaking, over the long-term, delight, happiness, and well-being correlate with mind-to-world correspondence, and general psychological dissonance correlates with a lack of mind-to-world correspondence. Hence, studying is important, as it directly optimizes your beliefs.

15. Looking at studying as a healthy sacrifice

Studying is good for all aspects of life, similar to exercise. Exercise benefits your life in various ways. Exercise is a sacrifice. Exercise may be difficult at times. But overall, exercise is a healthy sacrifice which produces many benefits.

In the same way, although studying in itself is pleasant, it may be regarded as a healthy sacrifice during the difficult times, when studying is found to be difficult. This healthy sacrifice of studying benefits your mind, which is even more important than your body. Since studying pertains to something that is more important than the body, studying is even more important than exercise.

Let this be motivation for you to activate your intelligence over and over again, knowing and trusting that the results of this exertion will improve the core of your being.

When we think of sacrifice, the quality of selflessness comes to mind. Now, the activity of studying—in itself, according to its definition—is one of the highest instances of selflessness. There is a difference between what studying is in itself and how people actually engage in the activity of studying. They may engage in studying only half-heartedly and with little intention to concentrate. But, as studying in itself represents a great instance of selflessness, a person participates in the quality of selflessness to the extent they execute the activity of studying according to its ideal form and principle.

Why, exactly, is studying an instance of selflessness? The explanation can trace to the following observations. (1) A person, in its essence, is its mind. (For example, in my essence, I am my mind, and in your essence, you are your mind.) (2) The self of a person is, roughly speaking, the person's perceiving mind, which is the perceiving and knowing subject. (This is almost the same as the previous premise.) (3) In acts of knowledge, the knowing subject encounters the knowable object, and knowledge arises in the unity between the two, as the subject comes to understand the object. This is where the subject transcends itself and meets the 'otherness' of the object. (4) Selflessness is just that—where the subject rises above itself, particularly for the sake of something noble, good, and beautiful. It was noted in (2) that the self of the person is basically the person's mind.

Therefore, it is shown that studying is an instance of selflessness, according to its very definition, since studying means coming to know things. For any individual person who engages in studying, studying will be an instance of selflessness to the extent of the depth and completeness with which the person encounters, beholds, and understands the objects of knowledge. Since selflessness is a core aspect of sacrifice, it is clear that studying is a healthy sacrifice, understood rightly.

The idea of this chapter harmonizes with our common sense and intuition. The life of Martin Luther King, Jr. may serve as an example. He contributed in a profound way to the healing of racial injustice. An important part of his success was his extensive knowledge in the subjects he studied. Let us imagine two points on the timeline, namely, point A before Dr. King entered college, and point B immediately after he offered his "I Have a Dream" speech in Washington D.C. at the Lincoln Memorial. If we are present with Dr. King at point A, it will be clear that in order for Dr. King to successfully reach point B with the greatest efficiency and harmony, he must execute his studies well and attain great levels in knowledge. Clearly, the activities of studying, between point A and point B, will be for him acts of selflessness and sacrifice, since his studies will empower him to contribute to the common good of humanity with extraordinary power and depth.

16. Activating your intuition

The process of studying should harmonize with your intuition. In calm discernment, let your intuition guide the way that you study. Why is this important? You can never *get rid of* your intuition. It will always be a part of your being. Essentially, your intuition is your deeper power of knowing, which can be active in low or high degrees of strength. So, if your studying does not harmonize with the power of your intuition, you will lack genuine alignment and resonance in your studies.

How do you harmonize your studies with your intuition? Become self-aware and make sure that you deeply believe in what you are doing. Only proceed with your studies when you believe that you are proceeding in the right manner. Determine whether you are on the right path, and if you are not, properly correct yourself, so that you authentically believe in what you do. Strive for peace of soul.

Knowledge may be divided into two kinds. The first kind is your opinions and beliefs. The second kind is your intuitive knowledge. Relative to each other, intuitive knowledge exists on a deeper plane in the mind, and opinions and beliefs exist on a shallower plane in the mind. Generally, opinions and beliefs arise from intuitive knowledge, but not the other way around: intuitive knowledge does not arise from opinions and beliefs. This is like how the leaves of a tree arise from the trunk and the branches, but the trunk and the branches do not arise from the leaves.

Your intuitive knowledge and the deep structure of your psychology are one and the same. Intuitive knowledge is active in a person to the extent that unity and harmony characterize the structure of the person's psychology. For this reason, virtue and intuitive knowledge are proportionate and mutually cause each other. That is, to the extent a person has virtue, to that extent the person has intuitive knowledge. To the extent the person has intuitive knowledge, to that extent the person has virtue. In addition, if a person activates virtue in themselves, that itself is to activate intuitive knowledge in themselves, for virtue causes intuitive knowledge to arise. Likewise, activating one's intuition is itself to cause virtue to increase in oneself, for intuition causes virtue to arise.

What is virtue? Virtue is the degree of unity characterizing the structure of one's deep psychology. This may also be known as the unity of the soul, although I am using the term 'deep psychology' in order to avoid any mysterious connotations of the word 'soul.' So, virtue is psychological unity, and vice is psychological disunity. Thus, virtue and vice are realities in an individual. They are objective and measurable.

Virtue and vice have multiple meanings. In one meaning of those terms, they are mere ideas, constructed in human culture, often to control people and keep people down. For example, virtue may be constructed to mean a set of qualities, which in the perspective of a group in power, render the majority of people obedient and unsophisticated. Although this is one possible sense of the terms virtue and vice, this is not the sense I am working with here in this chapter. Here, I am using the primary sense of virtue and vice—the objective structure of an individual's psychology. To the extent that the field of psychology is objective and valid, to that extent virtue and vice are objective and real, since these terms refer to the degree of coherence, unity, and harmony in the deep psychology of an individual.

Since virtue is proportionate to intuition, and since intuition leads one to discover and affirm true opinions and beliefs, this important conclusion follows: generally speaking, you will discover and maintain true beliefs and opinions to the extent that you gain virtue and avoid vice. Remember that virtue and vice refer to the unity and disunity, respectively, of your deep psychology. The main virtues are often regarded to be four: wisdom, justice, courage, and temperance. The corresponding vices are ignorance, injustice, cowardice, and intemperance. Therefore, like with anything in life when there is the question of attaining something good and worthwhile, the path to the goal must be authentic, solid, and true. In order to attain your potential in your studies, you must activate your intuition, and to active your intuition, you must have virtue in your soul, or equivalently, in your deep psychology. And you must remove vice—for example, ignorance, injustice, cowardice, and intemperance. This is good news and cause for optimism: although the path to success in your studies involves difficulty, it is something knowable and doable.

17. Wisely interpreting others' evaluations

It is important to understand that certain external evaluations of your work offered by certain groups, such as marks, ratings, scores, grades, and opinions, are just one among many measures of the quality of your work. They should be factored into the whole. They should be interpreted according to their actual nature and qualities, without giving them too little or too much weight. Some forms of external evaluation are more reliable than others.

Therefore, one must have the wisdom to understand when an external evaluation should be carefully incorporated, and when it should be taken lightly, or even respectfully set aside.

First, it may be noted that there are only a limited number of individuals or groups—not the entirety of humanity—that would give formal evaluations of your work. These evaluations may take many forms, such as grades and ratings. The individuals or groups in question probably do not represent the totality of reason. Their judgement is not infallible. They may be mistaken at times. It is possible that they missed the perception of some important component of the actual value of your work. Other individuals or groups, distinct from the ones presently evaluating your work, may see your work differently.

Second, your own judgement is also a valid measure. Trust that. Do you have an insight into the objective nature of the value of your work that others may be missing? Perhaps this unseen value will come to be appreciated in the near future, but not at present, due to various factors. In your judgement, how much are you learning? To what extent are you progressing in your goals? What is your independent evaluation of the matter? It may take great strength and courage to take seriously your independent evaluation of your work when it goes against others' evaluations.

Third, how your knowledge stacks up against other standards, besides those found in your immediate environment, is also a measure. For example, how does your knowledge of a subject stack up to the content of the Wikipedia article which deals with that subject? For example, it would be a pity, and an instance of delusion, if you got good grades in a certain area in school, but your knowledge was actually shallow and deficient compared to the information contained in an encyclopedia article, such as a Wikipedia or Brittanica article. In that case, you would falsely believe that you had deep knowledge of the subject. You would have little reason to be satisfied about the grades that your school institution gave you, if you had such shallow knowledge of the subject, after all—if having real knowledge is one of your values.

In this way, sometimes external evaluations are not critical enough of your work. If you accept such evaluations as authoritative, you may slow your progress. You may start to conform to those standards in a way that undermines your growth. This would happen if the standards in question actually run along a lower level of quality than what you are capable of and what you naturally would tend to envision.

Therefore, you must be mature and broad-minded when it comes to any kind of external evaluation offered by others. Do not let your judgement be insulated within the small box of your local environment. You should be aware of the general knowledge that humanity as a whole, as distinct from the particular groups or individuals in your local environment, has about a certain subject, and let that be an important standard in the back of your mind.

The mind has a nearly unlimited potential to grow, receive new information, and attain unexplored levels in learning. If you set your standards too low, those very standards may limit you, simply because you are not looking high enough. But if you look to higher standards, you may find yourself effortlessly expanding yourself to conform to those standards. Then, the standards in your immediate environment, when you return to consider them, may appear to be closer to child's play than before.

In your education, do not be afraid of external marks, such as grades. Be authentic. Study properly. And trust that the momentum of your authentic work will bring you to the right results in your education and life.

Grades are meant to be a marker of a separate, distinct thing— your work. Grades do not exist by themselves. Treating the grades as a substantial thing may be to fall into a black hole—a mere nothing. Grades are merely reactive things; they signify reactions, or responses, to your work.

Therefore, pursue substance and skill in your work, and satisfactory results and marks will tend to follow. Again, what are the purpose of scores and evaluations? To evaluate the level of substance, skill, and truth in your work. Therefore, go for that purpose directly.

Some evaluations of your work may truly and accurately point out its flaws and deficiencies. The key is to recognize this. One should have the right disposition—as part of one's character, at all times—in order to be receptive enough to recognize when a certain negative evaluation of one's work is true and should be processed with great care. This disposition may be characterized by the qualities of humility and receptiveness.

Humility signifies a correct and true understanding of oneself— not a false understanding. If you have X, Y, and Z qualities, then humility is to understand *that* you have X, Y, and Z qualities. Humility is having a correct judgement about your talents and limits, your good and bad qualities, your strengths and weaknesses. Humility is not primarily about emotions and attitudes.

Correct self-understanding is the actual virtue at play here when we discuss humility. The concept of humility came into play, we may infer, as a loose way of referring to the more primary virtue of correct self-understanding, since most people were found to believe themselves to be better than they were. Humility comes from the Latin word *humus*, which means ground. Since most people do not perceive some of the bad qualities they actually do have, most people have to get more down-to-earth in order to recognize these weaknesses and thus approach a more accurate self-understanding. But humility is not a complete representation of the virtue of correct self-understanding, since sometimes one must become more internally assertive, and grow closer to the sky, in order to recognize and appreciate the good qualities that one actually does have.

So, in order to recognize and skillfully integrate critical feedback and evaluations, one must have correct self-understanding, which is often termed humility. One belief that ruins correct self-understanding is the belief that one is the best in something. In fact, one is always a part in a whole. It is wise, I believe, to think that there are potentially *infinite* parts in the whole, and thus, that there will always be more skillful individuals than you in whatever area you are in. In your everyday experience, there are consistently examples and instances of superior talent and skill arising before you in various expressions. If you have this false belief that you are the best, you will miss all of them, and you may become stifled and inflated, missing out on upward trajectories of progress.

The reason that there are always examples and instances of superior talent and knowledge—in some respect, in some area—moving in front of you, is because life is a dynamic system, where every part complements and supports every other part, in some way. If you fail to understand the truth that you are a part, and not the whole, you will fail to flourish in the dynamic system of existence, which always transcends any particular individual and its understanding. You receive more strength and power, not less, if you have correct self-understanding and accurately understand the nature of yourself as a part, with your good and bad qualities, since your judgement will actually *correspond* to reality. If you believe yourself to be better than you are, your judgement will fail to correspond to reality—it will correspond to nothing, and it will be a lifeless delusion, lacking substance and power. Vitality, in part, emerges from the accuracy of one's understanding.

Vigilance is required. You may strongly feel that you do not think that you are the best in anything. But you may hold this belief subconsciously. And you may subconsciously believe that you are the best in some small area, in some little thing. Perhaps you may cling to this belief in reaction to confronting a major weakness of yours that was exposed during the course of your relations with others. In whatever place in your mind you believe that you are the best—even subconsciously—in that place, there is emptiness and lack of substance. Those false beliefs should be harmoniously replaced with correct self-understandings. To accurately recognize the virtue and strength you have, is not the same as believing you are the best. This is a subtle distinction, but this distinction is important.

In conclusion, wisely interpret others' evaluations. To do this, have a correct self-understanding of yourself. Understand your nature as a part in the whole. Understand accurately the qualities you have—the positive, the negative, and the grey. Then, you will have both a firm harmony and a receptiveness within yourself, enabling you to either (1) look beyond others' evaluations, (2) carefully integrate others' evaluations, or (3) do something in between, depending on the situation.

18. Balance in studying

There should be balance in your studying. You should know when to study more, and when to study less. It is important to maintain a pace that you can pleasantly keep.

One ideal, or benchmark, is that you feel that you could maintain your studying routine for fifty years without a problem, since it is pleasant.

There is a certain misunderstanding that the greatest productivity in studying occurs when you are nearly out of breath, huffing and puffing, sweating, and feeling the pain of the process. This is false. That state of being cannot generally be sustained. It will naturally be followed with the proportionate reaction—an intense inclination to relax, put away the books, and do something else. In fact, you may be remarking about how praiseworthily and intensely you studied the day before, only while you are relaxing on a chair, not doing any studying now. Whereas, is there not equal reason to criticize yourself for your current inactivity? So, the point is clear: If you had engaged in moderate, sustainable studying the day before, you would have found it similarly pleasant to study today. In the end, proceeding down this middle path will be more productive, yet in a low-key manner, as if nothing special is going on.

Studying with balance allows you to consistently output the highest levels of productivity, yet all the while maintaining ease and enjoyment in the process. There is no burnout, since you find the activity to be pleasant. With this method, you continue with ease at those points when you might have long abandoned the activity had you been exerting too much effort, in a disordered manner, in a short period of time.

19. Using your imagination when writing

Your imagination is something that is very powerful. There may be a tendency to dismiss the significance of the imagination, due to the idea that the imagination is the realm of your own thought, instead of being an actual reality. Now, it is true that your imagination is the realm of your thought, but this does not mean that it does not have much importance.

Here is an analogy. There is a certain town. In the middle of the town, there is a great, shared marketplace, where people buy and sell food and other goods and services. There are also many homes around the marketplace. The people live in their homes and then come to the marketplace, interacting with each other in various ways. The homes are important, too, even though they are not the places of the town's shared interactions and main activity. Each person must take good care of their home. Significant family activity occurs in the homes.

With this analogy, the homes represent people's imaginations, and the marketplace represents the concrete, actual world, common to everyone's experience. It would be a terrible and costly mistake to neglect the right use of one's home. An important and fundamental part of one's life would not be in right order, and bad effects would arise in one's life and activity. In a similar way, the imagination forms an important part of one's nature as an intelligent being. If the imagination is neglected and not rightly used, suboptimal effects may arise in one's life and activity. The imagination is a place of possibility from which we can develop ideas that will eventually impact the world.

Therefore, your imagination is very important, and to neglect its fruitful use is to miss out on one's full functioning and potential as a human being. Obviously, we should rightly develop and use our minds to a full extent, not merely in a fractional way. In fact, notice that you have to use your imagination to see what it would be like to use more of your mind. See how the imagination is critical in transitioning to a potentially improved state of being.

As a certain part of the mind, the imagination is important, just as eating is important, even though eating is not the same as contributing to the common good. The activity of eating is a subjective experience, and the state of the common community is something that is objective. The imagination is subjective, and the actual world is objective.

In a larger way of looking at it, there is only the objective. The imagination is also a small, objective part of the objective, actual world, except that only the individual person has access to this small part of the objective world. Likewise, only you have access to the immediate experience and activity of tasting your meal, but the meal, and the activity of your tasting it, are small parts of the objective world.

So, even though your imagination is subjective, it is still important. One's imagination is important, even though it is not as important as the actual, objective world. The subjective is included within the objective. The imagination of each person is a certain, objective part, with its properties and qualities, of the total, objective world. If each person's imagination was *not* part of the objective world, there would be no possibility of it having any bearing on the objective world. Any connection between one's imagination and the objective world would be impossible, if each person's imagination was not a small, objective part of the objective world.

For example, the person who imagined and invented the first horse carriage could never have brought the idea into existence, for the benefit of the world, if there was no objective connection between that person's imagination and the objective world. Since there *is* such an objective connection, it must be acknowledged that the person's imagination is also an objective part of the objective world, even though that part is very small compared to the whole world.

This shows that your imagination is something meaningful. When you use and develop your imagination, you are doing something meaningful. It is meaningful because it is something real.

Your imagination is to be rightly used in your writing. Seek to explore. If you are writing fiction, you may imagine the characters, the scenes, the plot, and the interactions as much as possible *before* writing down the material. This may endow the writing process with more clarity and form. You may feel more connected to something substantial during the writing process.

In all kinds of writing, not just fiction, it will be important to use and explore your imagination. In this way, you will be activating more of your potential as an intelligent being.

20. Contemplating one point deeply

One strategy when engaging with your study material is to spend a long time on a single point, entering deeply into the field of your study material through a prolonged contemplation of that one point. This strategy is like digging a deep well in one place on the ground, and continuing to dig, and dig, and dig, as you enter deeper into the earth. In this analogy, the entire study material is like the field of earth that surrounds the place where you are digging, and the place where you dig the well represents the single entry point into the material. This point may be an important aspect of the material; it may be a major theme; it may be a thesis. It will be anything that has particular significance in light of the whole material. So, you hold onto that one point and contemplate deeply on it. Eventually, you will reach deeper levels of understanding.

Since all of the points of the study material are interconnected, once you attain a deep understanding of that one point, you automatically encounter a deeper understanding of some of the related points. You find that the other points are easier to understand, since you tapped into the deep waters, the gold, of the first point.

This strategy helps you avoid just wandering around the earthen field, not digging anywhere in particular. You might notice all of the points that you eventually have to cover and become frustrated. Your attention is scattered all over the place, and you grow to despise and hate the process of studying. This is not a skillful approach to studying. Instead, when you dig deep into one, particular point, you allow your subconscious mind to receive all kinds of information, and it becomes easier to intuitively process the material and connect the dots.

Here is a related example. Suppose Michael is studying computer hardware in high school. He never learned the formal knowledge of this subject, but many of the other students already had some degree of technical knowledge of various aspects of the subject. However, Michael's father was a computer engineer, and Michael recalls the times in his early childhood when computers would be all around the family living room, and Michael would spend hours looking at the computers and appreciating the connection between his father and the computer hardware. Now, once Michael begins his high school class, he finds it extraordinarily easy and intuitive to learn the material and piece together the information. The other students initially have a slight advantage in technical comprehension of the material, but soon, Michael excels all the other students, due to the deep, immediate connection to the material he had in the core of his being.

Now, when you spend a long time deeply contemplating a single, important point in the material, bringing it into the space of your own being, you are approaching the state of Michael, who had that deep connection to computer hardware due to his direct, sustained, and personal exposure to his father's engagement with computers. When you stick with that single point, you forge a personal connection to the material in your very being. You approach a kind of unity with the material. Then, you start to speak with experience when you discuss various aspects of the material, because you begin to consult your immediate encounter with the material, instead of working with shallow concepts that have not been internalized deeply.

If you deeply understand one point, you will run into other points on that deeper plane of understanding. Momentum is created.

In summary, the strategy is this: Select a single point in the material, and contemplate it deeply. Then, the rest of the material will tend to open up to you. At least, it will become more accessible to your understanding, since you have pierced the ground through your sustained contemplation; you have entered the underlying field, or grid, of the material.

This strategy works due to the premise that all of the points of the material tend to be interconnected. For this strategy to work best, you have to select an important point, a significant point, for your deep contemplation.

21. Trusting in the power of your mind

At times, you may feel that you will not be able to balance and coordinate the various subjects you are studying. Ideally, it is good to have order and clarity in all aspects of your studies. However, suppose you are balancing many different projects at the same time, and you find it difficult to consciously process all those variables at once. You may feel inclined to eliminate your involvement in some of the projects in order to regain simplicity and a conscious feeling of control. This may be the right approach.

However, it is also possible that there is another way forward. You may trust in your subconscious intuition to process all of the relevant information, as you proceed from one subject to another, or one project to another, making bits of progress with the work, even though you may be unable to consciously connect all the dots. Trust that the deeper layers of your mind will be able to put the pieces together, particularly if you allow yourself enough time to rest and engage in calm reflection.

This strategy is based on the principle that there is a distinction between your surface consciousness and your subconsciousness, and that the surface consciousness may not be aware of the powers of the subconsciousness to process activities and handle multiple streams of information. This is similar to the phenomenon where after a restful and rejuvenating sleep, new clarity arises about the obstacles one is navigating, and one receives energy to resolve the obstacles and reach solutions.

In order to tap into this latent potency of your mind during the day, it is necessary to preserve a degree of harmony and calm in your being, even if you are facing a multitude of tasks. A good analogy is a swimming pool. Many different objects can be floating on the water and even moving beneath the water surface. The pool itself can handle all of this; it simply contains all of them and itself remains unaffected. Now, you must become like the mass of water which easily contains all of the pool objects without become destabilized.

Notice that in order to do this, your intention, in the beginning, is not, "I intend to process all of these tasks now," but rather, "I intend to settle into a firm foundation, which exists at a deeper level than these tasks, and from which I can successfully process all of them."

22. Not letting the perfect be the enemy of the good

It is important to not let the perfect be the enemy of the good.

This does not mean that you should not let perfection be your goal. You should—in the right way. The way should be a harmonious and smooth way, not a stressful and incapacitating way.

The advice offered is to not let the perfect be the *enemy* of the good. This does not mean that perfection is not to be within your sights.

This is about *iteration* and smooth progress. Allow yourself to create something, and let it be imperfect. At least you have moved forward one step, and this is a big accomplishment. Once *something* is set down, you can improve it.

There is a difference between perfection and your *concept* of perfection. Perfection can come about unexpectedly. For example, you are walking one day under the blue sky, and the sun is shining behind some beautiful clouds. You suddenly have the conviction, "Ah, this is perfect." See how perfection is a reality that operates independently of your expectation.

The *concepts* of perfection that people have can be debilitating. They can entirely stop one's progress. For example, if someone's self-image of themselves is mixed with even a little bit of a lack of appreciation for their own actual worth, then their concepts of perfection may actually carry some degree of error and disorder. They may subconsciously carry some elements of personal disadvantage into their concepts of perfection, falsely thinking that their *concepts* of perfection actually signify, and point to, real perfection.

Actualize concrete steps toward the *good*, and be mindful about your concepts of perfection. Then, through a slow and smooth process, filled with harmony and balance, move toward perfection. The path toward perfection should be one of satisfaction and joy, not of tightness, constriction, stress, and disorder.

Perhaps you have had the experience when, after an event has occurred, you judge the event to have been more or less perfect, or to have exhibited a certain degree of perfection. However, while you were in the event, and during the time before the event started, your vision about what you were trying to do was very moderate and natural. It is likely the case that there was fluidity and harmony between your vision and your nature and emotions, such that a state of flow could arise in your activity. Here, there was a vision of the *good* during the activity, and after the event ended, there was a judgement that the event was *perfect*.

Two conclusions arise. First, note that the judgement that the event was perfect is likely to be inaccurate. By perfect, we really mean that the event was sufficiently good and exceeded most or all of our expectations. If we notate the event as sufficiently good instead of as perfect, we will allow ourselves to recognize the space for progress, and we will not have the mistaken belief that we have attained perfection. This mistaken belief can produce constriction and obstacles, since by definition, there is no way to rise higher than what is already perfect. Also, our standards of evaluation may become misaligned, since unobserved inadequacies and imperfections that *were* in the event which we called perfect will then be consciously or subconsciously lumped into our concept of what perfection is.

The second conclusion is that our reasonable visions of the good are what often produce our subjective *experiences* of perfection.

Actualizing this approach—having reasonable visions of the good in the short-term—is consistent with consciously aiming for perfection over the long-term in a steady and progressive manner.

23. Music as an aid

Intelligently using music during your studies can be a good help. Music can uplift your mood and even energize you. Particularly, music that is purely instrumental, without human voice, can engage with more of the subconscious aspect of the mind. Instrumental music may be more compatible with studying and focus. You can think of the music to be like a background river, whose current helps you to be propelled forward in your studies.

It is important to set aside some time to think about precisely this point: What music will benefit me the most in my studies? (This question will apply for those times when you judge that music will be useful to use in your studies; such times may be more or less in your studies, depending on your nature and circumstances.) It will be important to get the answer right to this question, since the type of music will have a big impact on your studies. Many people prefer ambient kinds of music that set an ethereal mood to the study space. You can use trial and error to identify effective forms of music for your studies.

When should you use music in your studies? Perhaps when you know you need to study, but find it difficult to do so; your surface consciousness is somehow inclined to do something else. At such times, you might put on the music that you have pre-selected and smoothly merge into the sound of the music, allowing the music to be a current to help propel you forward and increase your enjoyment of the study process.

23. Music as an aid

Music is powerful. It can inspire. It can rejuvenate. Music is to be used with wisdom, contributing to the sharpness and vitality of your studies.

24. Meditation for improved studying

The quality of your consciousness will determine the quality of the thoughts you have. Meditation will improve the quality of your consciousness, leading to better thoughts, and thus, more success in your studies.

How does meditation, done rightly and with intelligence, improve the quality of your consciousness? Meditation helps your mind to recollect itself, become settled, and become more unified. Meditation helps you to feel and achieve more unity in your consciousness, instead of being scattered, distracted, and destabilized. This makes a large difference in the quality of your studies.

There are many effective methods of meditation for this purpose. It is important to have a goal for your meditation. This brings clarity to your meditation and helps you regroup if you get distracted in your meditation.

Now, one method is to sit in stillness. (Or, you may be still mentally, if you are standing or moving.) In this method of sitting in stillness, you have the goal of letting your thoughts settle and attaining conscious peace and unity in your mind.

Another method is to meditate on a particular archetype, such as peace, strength, space, harmony, intelligence, life, or happiness. Meditating on such archetypes brings clarity and depth to your mind. You may consider the particular situation you happen to be in, and then identify the archetype which stands in contrast to any negative quality characterizing the situation. For example, if *stress* is the dominant quality at a particular time, let your archetype for meditation be *peace*. If *confusion* arises, let your archetype be *intelligence*. If *pettiness* is a negative quality in the situation in which you find yourself, then you can meditate on *profundity*.

If you hold still, in a seated position, with your eyes closed, with conscious awareness, for some time, then the energies of your mind and body will become recollected to some extent. Then, you will be in more balance. You will find more clarity in your mind. This clarity will make studying easier. This is an effective method.

Indeed, it is important to have a goal for your meditation. This contributes to your meditation being an act of autonomy and self-responsibility, in which you have full ownership over the activity, and in which your executive intelligence presides over the meditation like a charioteer or monarch. In general, you can let your goal be to attain clarity and harmony in your mind. These qualities—clarity and harmony—are advantageous to aim for, since they are both spiritual and not spiritual. In other words, no rational being, of whatever worldview, will reasonably deny that having clarity and harmony in one's mind is a good thing. At the same time, if any spiritual outlook or starting premises are admitted, the qualities of clarity and harmony will always be among the highest spiritual archetypes possible. Yet the qualities of clarity and harmony are not mysterious or rationally problematic. Therefore, if you make the goal of your meditation to attain clarity and harmony, you maintain both the reasonableness of the meditation and the capacity to maximize the possible potential of meditation as an activity. This kind of meditation will help your studies.

25. Run your technology; do not let it run you

Technology may be good or bad, depending on its nature, purpose, and how it is used. In general, I believe it is important that you *run the technology*, instead of permitting the technology *to run you*.

This may require spending more time with your technology, such as phones and computers, to set them up this way. A complete knowledge of your technological hardware and software programs and applications will be important in order to understand the technology, to run it, to control it, and to have power over it, so that you ensure that it benefits you in the proper ways.

First, identify what your goals are and what you want to do. Then, second, set up your technology to help you achieve your goals. Make sure that you spend time thinking about your goals, so that you ensure that the goals you set up are the products of your independent, intellectual activity, instead of just picking them up from somewhere else, not really checking whether the goals harmonize with your being. Then, set up, configure, and use your technology to help you achieve those goals.

What you want to avoid is letting your technology control you, where you are passive and mentally dormant. For example, suppose you see your phone and then pick it up. But, you never made the actual decision to use your phone. You just picked it up out of habit, to do something, perhaps reacting to an inner feeling of emptiness and subconsciously wanting some kind of stimulation. Then, you react to the material and content that you just happen to encounter on the device. An hour passes by, and you feel dazed and tired by the end. You do not feel satisfied with yourself either.

The better scenario is where you have an intention to do something. This intention you certify with your intelligence—you stand behind it with your entire being. Then, you pick up your phone to accomplish that task. This is productivity. This is good use of technology, where the technology serves your highest good.

A massive error is to misunderstand the distinction between the highest possible limit of technology and your organic nature as a conscious human being. There are some things that technology will never do. One of those things is: to understand *for* you. The power of your understanding, the act of understanding, is something that pertains to the core of your being. No possible technology will, or could, do this, or replace this. You have to understand things *for yourself.* Technology can present to you masses of excellent and true information, but it cannot understand the information for you. You must understand the information. The act of understanding, the act of knowledge, will always be a property of your identity, and never the identity of any technology hardware or technology software. The act of organizing your understanding, and the act of instantiating harmony and coherence in your consciousness, will also be perpetual properties of your own identity.

Hypothetically, there are potential forms of technology that will organize some material in your mind for you. However, one attribute of every individual consciousness is that there is always an answer, and a pathway, associated with the question, "What is the nature of the conscious knower or perceiver?" Consciousness, I believe, is ultimately a fractal thing, and so the inquiry into the nature of the conscious knower is an unending inquiry; it leads to deeper regions of consciousness without end. (Anyone can experiment with this inquiry and investigation into the nature of the conscious knower, into the question, "What is that which knows?")

So, the mental material that this hypothetical technology could organize for you—and even produce, whereby it would be called a second mind—would always exist as an object in consciousness, and only on a certain, determinate layer in consciousness. Since the inquiry into the subject of consciousness can always be made and is always unending, this critical conclusion arises: *there will always be a distinction between technology and your core essence.*

Thus, we see that one of the ultimate questions surrounding technology would become: "Can technology absorb my substantial identity as a thinking, conscious, intelligent being?" In terms of practical functionality, the answer may be yes, if humans let themselves move into mental dormancy. However, in terms of substantial reality, it is impossible that one's identity as a conscious, intelligent substance could ever be replaced, displaced, or absorbed in its *being* (although again, it may so in practice). This is like how the number 35 can never become the number 36, although in practice, the number 35 may be exclusively used in a society, where it would be as if the number 36 does not exist. But it does exist; it is just not used. The number 35 represents technology; the number 36 represents the human identity as a substance with consciousness.

As of the publication of this book in 2025, a reasonable view is that artificial general intelligence, AGI, both is possible and will be the most important instance of technology for the next several centuries, and presumably, for thousands of years, given the primacy of intelligence. We can estimate that a world with AGI will eventually be a world where humans have immediate access to a robust theory of everything—that is, to an extensive and accurate explanation and account of the nature of reality, which would include physics and ontology. But the AGI could not understand that information *for* us. We would have to understand it. Thus, *an individual's own act of understanding* is something that technology will never be able to do or replace, even in a billion years.[1]

The conclusion is that you should develop your understanding and work on your *power of knowing* as something that will never be displaced by technology. When you work on this, you will be working on something that will be just as objectively valuable now as it will be in 5,000 years. Presumably, the *perceived* value of one's power of understanding will only increase when the capacities of technology increase in society. It is good to seek to understand what it is to *know* something. There will always be a distinction between technology, even in its highest possible modes and instances, and the power of your own act of understanding.

---

[1] Ultimately, the reason for this traces to the following, I believe. This is a distinct matter and consideration, which I do not wish to include in the main text, since it involves premises that are less easily accepted. The *act of understanding* is linked to the *conscious knower*, the inquiry into which, I have offered above, is fractal in nature. What is experienced as the conscious knower, in every individual consciousness, is, I offer, ultimately to be regarded as tracing to the common and objective cosmic singularity, the one. The cosmic singularity is uncreated, whereas all technology, by definition, is created. Hence, there is a categorical distinction between the two. Every node of consciousness is a certain, differentiated instantiation of the uncreated cosmic singularity. Thus, each node of consciousness is uncreated in its core essence, whereas any instance of technology is created. (The word 'technology' traces to the Greek word 'techne,' which traces to the idea of making or creating something.)

26. The method of asking questions

If you are entering a subject for the first time, or even just seeking to gain more knowledge in a subject that you have already worked with, a good starting method is to contemplate questions you naturally have about the subject, before simply reading the information and putative answers in other, established resources.

This requires a high level of self-trust and self-compassion, as the questions you have about the subject may feel childish or rudimentary—but in fact, they are probably not. The first principles of every subject deal with fundamental things of profound importance that many people mistakenly take for granted.

Even if your questions about a subject *are* childish and rudimentary, that is not a reason to abandon this process. The fact that your intellect genuinely produced these questions indicates that, for you, these are areas in which study and investigation will benefit you. In order to reap these benefits, you just have to overcome your pride and respectfully work with your questions.

In addition, if you enter into the subject matter through the doorway of your own questions, instead of through the doorway of other starting points, your learning process will feel more organic and grounded. This is because your questions were acts of *your own* intelligence. Compare this to the other method, where you enter into the subject matter through the doorway of starting points that are *not* acts of your own intelligence. It is simple: in one method, the starting points of learning necessarily resonate with your nature and disposition; in the other method, they will not necessarily do so, and they may feel distant and unclear.

This method requires more discipline and self-responsibility, since you are becoming the executive officer in your learning process, instead of just taking a backseat and permitting the way you begin to think about a subject to be formed by others. But your study process will become more efficient, since you are entering the subject through pathways that are natural and intuitive. The price to pay is overcoming your pride, as you gently and patiently work with your questions in the beginning that may feel foolish.

This method of asking questions is consistent with reading anything and everything about a subject. It is just that you take your own questions seriously, actualizing them in your study process, and you do so in the beginning, transforming the entire subsequent learning process into something that resonates with you.

27. Studying is a service to humanity; it is compassion

Have you ever thought of studying as an act of compassion? It actually is, if you carefully think about it.

What is compassion? Compassion is to open your heart to the other. Compassion is to expand your mind, your consciousness, to deeply understand and have sympathy for others. Compassion is to see the world through the eyes of another, and thus, to empathize with that person. Thus, compassion is a form of expanded knowledge—it is knowledge that includes the perspective of the other person, or group of people, as much as possible.

Imagine that each person's mind is represented by a circle. All of the circles, all the billions of them, are located within a huge, mega circle. The size of the circle represents the person's understanding. Having compassion for another is where the circle of one person encompasses the circle of another, to a sufficient extent.

Well, this is what studying and learning are. To study is to expand one's circle. Thus, studying is compassion. It is a service to humanity. The mind is opened to new knowledge and realities. The mind becomes aware of more perspectives.

War happens because either side failed to do enough studying. That is, war happens when there is not enough rational competence to resolve the issues between the two sides, using reason and verbal communication. Thus, war is a failure of the intelligence. Through studying and learning, war may be avoided. This shows that when you study, you contribute to a world of harmony, besides contributing to harmony and success for yourself and various communities in all kinds of other ways.

In order to sow peace where there is discord and disorder, one must understand how. One must have the knowledge. Studying is the process of getting this knowledge. Without knowledge, and thus, without right study, it will be difficult to improve the state of the world.

You will be motivated by reflecting on the profound nature of studying and the way that studying, in part, is an expression of compassion for humanity. Studying is a deeply meaningful activity.

www.ingramcontent.com/pod-product-compliance
Lightning Source LLC
LaVergne TN
LVHW091229080426
835509LV00009B/1216